BOOK HOUSE

BEASTLY
SCIENCE

MAMMAL MECHANICS

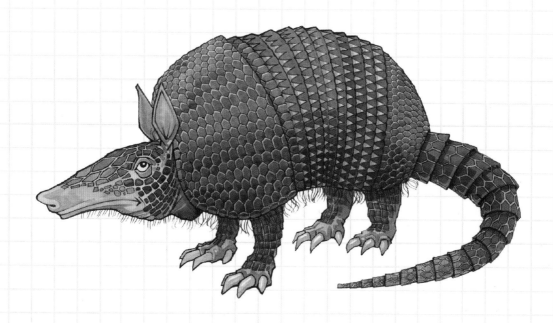

ILLUSTRATED BY
DAVID ANTRAM

WRITTEN BY
JOHN TOWNSEND

Author:

JOHN TOWNSEND worked as a Secondary School teacher before becoming a full time writer of children's books and a writer-in-residence in a primary school tree-house. He specialises in fun, exciting information books for reluctant readers, as well as fast-paced fiction, reading schemes and 'fiction with facts' books. He visits schools around the country to encourage excitement in all aspects of reading and writing. He has recently written 12 plays based on Salariya's *You Wouldn't Want To Be* series that have been uploaded to the company's new website for use in classrooms.

Artist:

DAVID ANTRAM studied at Eastbourne College of Art and then worked in advertising for fifteen years before becoming a full-time artist. He has since illustrated many popular information books for children and young adults, including more than 60 titles in the bestselling *You Wouldn't Want To Be* series.

Editor: **NICK PIERCE**

Published in Great Britain in MMXVIII by
Book House, an imprint of
The Salariya Book Company Ltd
25 Marlborough Place, Brighton BN1 1UB
www.salariya.com

ISBN: 978-1-912233-44-1

SALARIYA

1 3 5 7 9 8 6 4 2

A CIP catalogue record for this book is available from the British Library.

Printed and bound in China.

Visit our website at **www.salariya.com**

PAPER FROM
SUSTAINABLE
FORESTS

CONTENTS PAGE

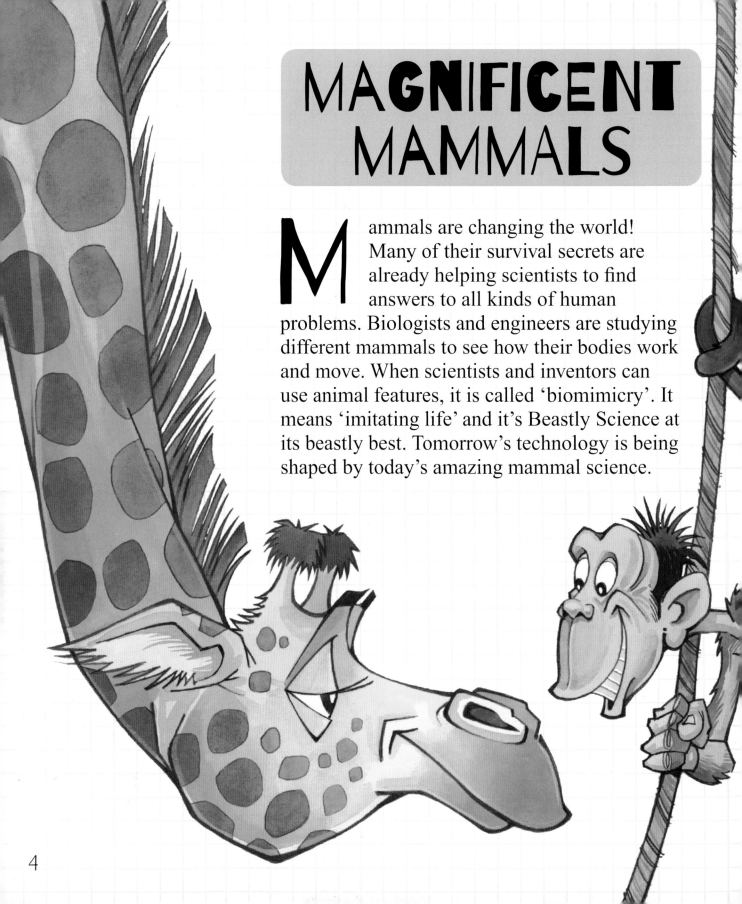

MAGNIFICENT MAMMALS

Mammals are changing the world! Many of their survival secrets are already helping scientists to find answers to all kinds of human problems. Biologists and engineers are studying different mammals to see how their bodies work and move. When scientists and inventors can use animal features, it is called 'biomimicry'. It means 'imitating life' and it's Beastly Science at its beastly best. Tomorrow's technology is being shaped by today's amazing mammal science.

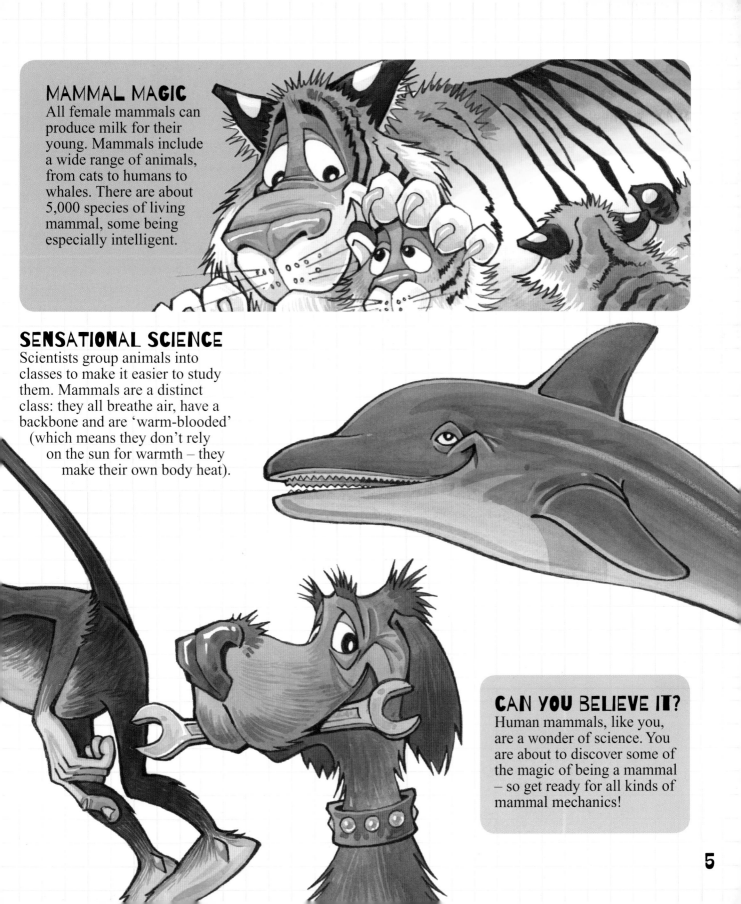

MAMMAL MAGIC

All female mammals can produce milk for their young. Mammals include a wide range of animals, from cats to humans to whales. There are about 5,000 species of living mammal, some being especially intelligent.

SENSATIONAL SCIENCE

Scientists group animals into classes to make it easier to study them. Mammals are a distinct class: they all breathe air, have a backbone and are 'warm-blooded' (which means they don't rely on the sun for warmth – they make their own body heat).

CAN YOU BELIEVE IT?

Human mammals, like you, are a wonder of science. You are about to discover some of the magic of being a mammal – so get ready for all kinds of mammal mechanics!

5

BAT SCIENCE

Bats are the only flying mammal. There are over 1,000 different kinds. The smallest bat, often known as the bumblebee bat, is not much bigger than a bee. The largest is the giant golden crowned flying fox, with a massive wingspan of 1.7 metres (5.5 feet).

Bats are nocturnal so they have to find their way in total darkness. They need to 'see' very well to catch prey and to avoid bumping into things. Oddly, it's their large super-ears that help them to do so.

FACT FILE

- Sound is energy made by vibrations which makes air particles move about. As these particles bump into other ones, they create sound waves. Fast vibrations sound like a high note. Slow vibrations make a low note.

- Sounds made by bats are usually so highly pitched that we can't hear them.

- Bats use their own sound waves to help them find their way around. This is called 'echolocation'.

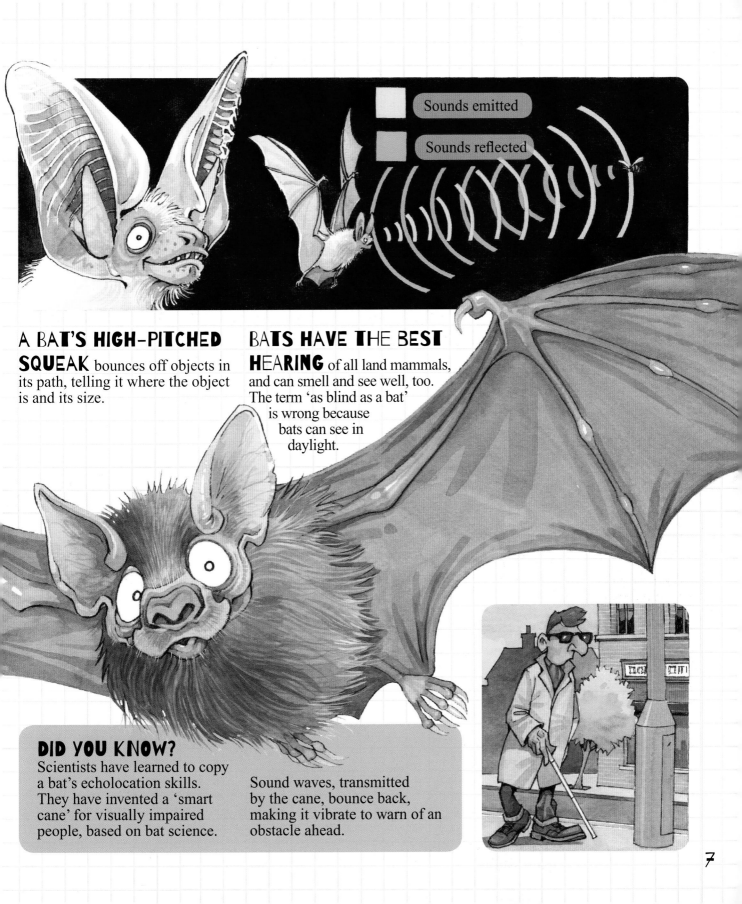

Sounds emitted

Sounds reflected

A BAT'S HIGH-PITCHED
SQUEAK bounces off objects in its path, telling it where the object is and its size.

BATS HAVE THE BEST
HEARING of all land mammals, and can smell and see well, too. The term 'as blind as a bat' is wrong because bats can see in daylight.

DID YOU KNOW?
Scientists have learned to copy a bat's echolocation skills. They have invented a 'smart cane' for visually impaired people, based on bat science.

Sound waves, transmitted by the cane, bounce back, making it vibrate to warn of an obstacle ahead.

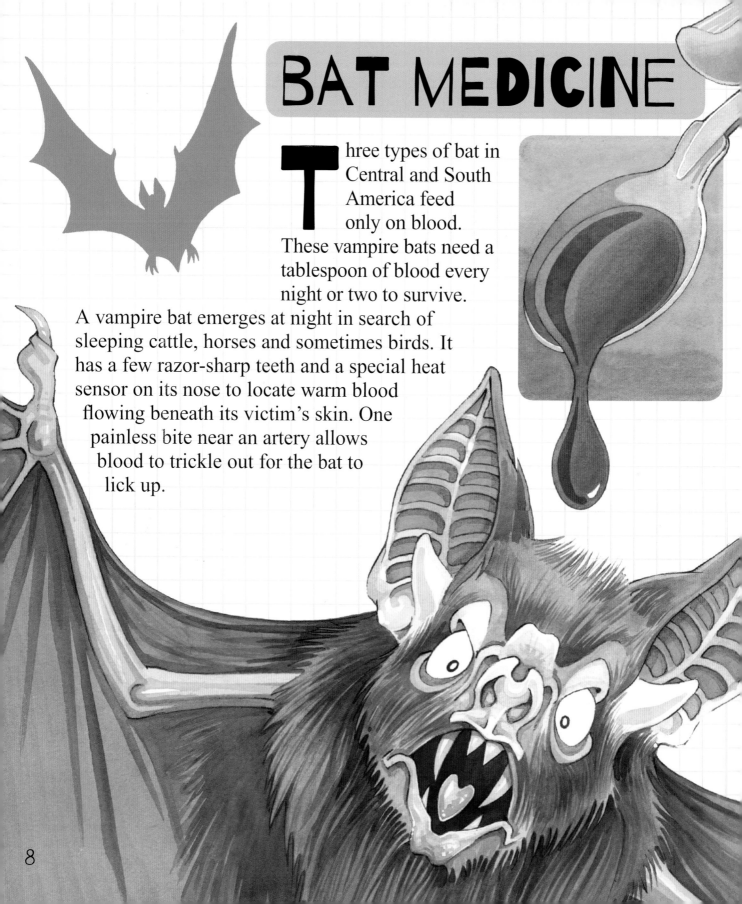

BAT MEDICINE

Three types of bat in Central and South America feed only on blood. These vampire bats need a tablespoon of blood every night or two to survive.

A vampire bat emerges at night in search of sleeping cattle, horses and sometimes birds. It has a few razor-sharp teeth and a special heat sensor on its nose to locate warm blood flowing beneath its victim's skin. One painless bite near an artery allows blood to trickle out for the bat to lick up.

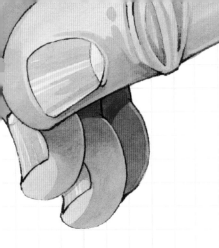

A CHEMICAL IN THE BATS' SALIVA stops blood from clotting and keeps it flowing. Scientists have been working with vampire bat saliva in medical research. It can be used to help increase the blood flow in patients suffering with strokes or heart disease.

A DRUG NOW BEING DEVELOPED has the scary-sounding name of Draculin. This blood-thinning drug is injected into patients to dissolve blood clots in the brain that would starve it of oxygen and cause a stroke. Draculin keeps the blood from clotting. It may seem batty… but the scary-looking vampire bat could actually turn out to be a life-saver after all.

FACT FILE

- A vampire bat is only about 9 cm (3.5 in) long and has a wingspan of 18 cm (7 in). It usually weighs about 25 to 40 grams (0.8 to 1.4 oz), but is heavier after it feeds.

- In one year a whole colony of over 1,000 vampire bats could drink cow-fulls of blood – without any of the cows even knowing.

- Scientists call a liquid blood diet 'hematophagy'… vampire bats just call it 'delicious'!

ROBO BATS

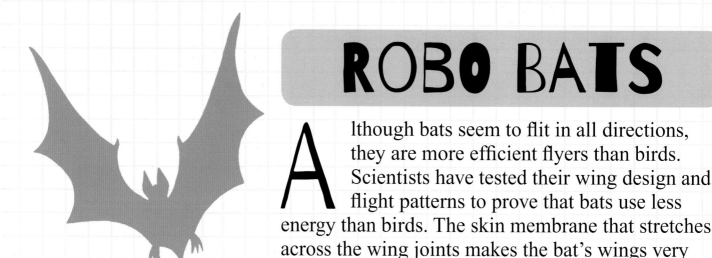

Although bats seem to flit in all directions, they are more efficient flyers than birds. Scientists have tested their wing design and flight patterns to prove that bats use less energy than birds. The skin membrane that stretches across the wing joints makes the bat's wings very flexible, and creates more lift, less drag and greater manoeuvrability. Can engineers make a machine that flies as well as a bat?

MEET COM-BAT – the United States military mini spy plane. Fitted with a solar panel in its 'head', the 15 cm (6-inch) COM-BAT has wings shaped like those of a bat. This spy plane can collect visual surveillance data as well as sounds and smells, while running on only 1 watt of power.

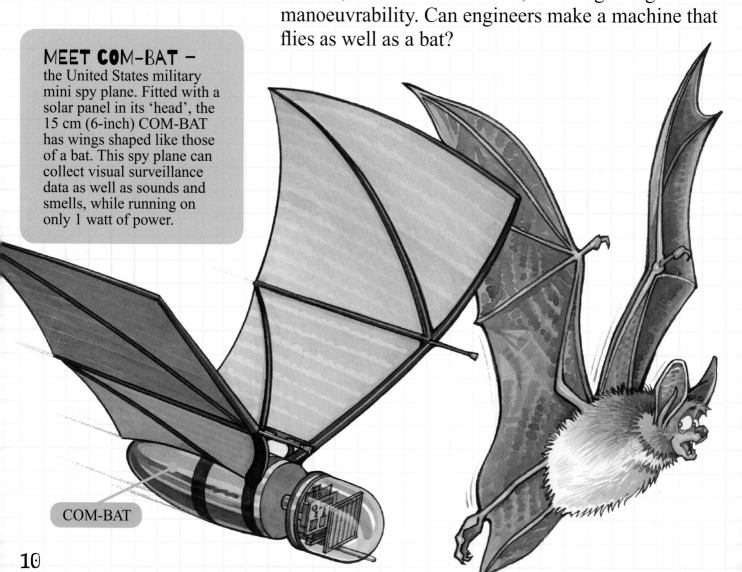

COM-BAT

NOW MEET BAT-BOT

Its design makes it less likely to be blown off course like a normal drone, with its bulky spinning rotors. Fitted with a camera, Bat-Bot could soon monitor construction sites, dangerous areas and disaster zones.

BAT-BOT only weighs 93 grams (3.3 ounces). It has nine joints in each wing and adjustable legs to help it steer. The bat robot flaps its wings for aerial manoeuvres or glides to save energy, and can even dive-bomb. It can't yet perch upside down just like a real bat. That's batty but brilliant science!

BAT-BOT

CAT SCIENCE

Cats have very good night vision, and are the source of an invention that helps drivers see unlit roads at night.

Percy Shaw (1890-1976) was an inventor and businessman. In 1933, Shaw was driving along a winding road on a foggy night and was saved from going into a ditch by a cat beside the road, whose eyes reflected his car's headlights. Percy had a brainwave. Using 'light-reflection science', he began making glass reflectors or 'cats' eyes' to mark out roads. This invention made Shaw his fortune. He set up a company to manufacture 'cats' eyes' in 1935 and received an OBE in 1965 for his contribution to making driving at night a safer and easier experience.

FACT FILE

- Unlike humans, cats have a thin vertical pupil that opens and closes very fast. This allows a cat's eyes to adjust more quickly from light to dark. They can see in the dark much better than us.

- A cat's eye has six to eight times more rod cells than a human's eye. These extra rod cells allow cats to see and sense motion in the dark much better than we can. That's why they are skilful night hunters

- White cats with blue eyes are usually deaf. If a cat is white and has only one blue eye, it will likely be deaf on that side too.

Percy Shaw

SIMPLE SCIENCE

At the back of a cat's eye, is a reflective layer called the tapetum lucidum (Latin: 'bright carpet'). This is found in many nocturnal animals with good night vision and is why a cat's eyes shine brightly when a light catches them in the dark.

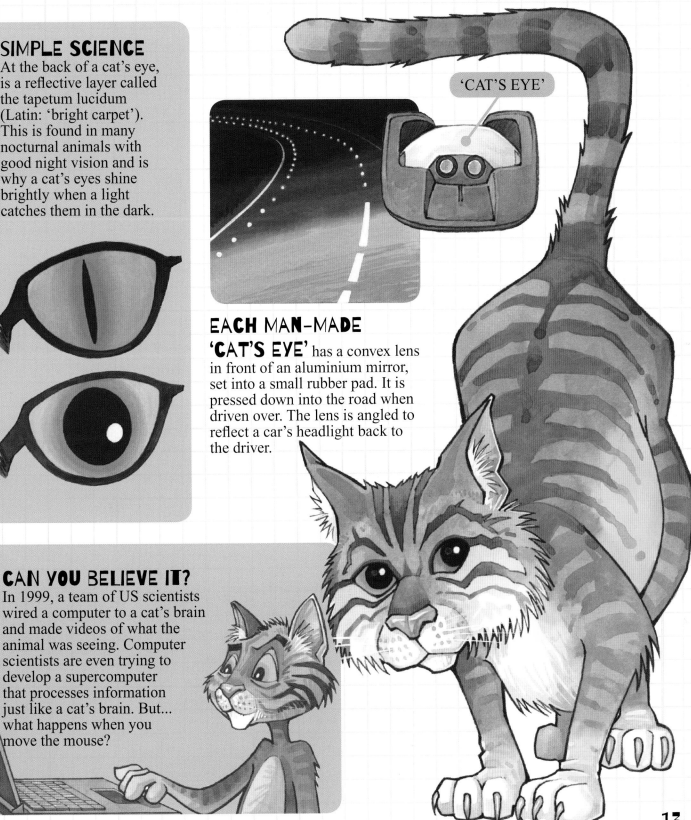

'CAT'S EYE'

EACH MAN-MADE 'CAT'S EYE' has a convex lens in front of an aluminium mirror, set into a small rubber pad. It is pressed down into the road when driven over. The lens is angled to reflect a car's headlight back to the driver.

CAN YOU BELIEVE IT?

In 1999, a team of US scientists wired a computer to a cat's brain and made videos of what the animal was seeing. Computer scientists are even trying to develop a supercomputer that processes information just like a cat's brain. But... what happens when you move the mouse?

13

NAKED MOLE RAT SCIENCE

T his strange little rodent is intriguing scientists, who think some of its secrets could be of help to humans. Scientists believe these odd creatures can survive without oxygen, by switching to a different 'fuel' to create energy in their bodies. Living in deep, cramped burrows, these mole rats don't get enough oxygen to breathe but keep alive by somehow using fructose (fruit sugar) in their bodies.

FACT FILE

- A naked mole rat is a pink, wrinkly, hairless rodent, not much bigger than a mouse. But it is neither a mole, nor a rat.

- Like a mole, the naked mole rat lives underground in parts of East Africa.

- Naked mole rats don't feel pain, are mostly resistant to cancer and can live ten times longer than a mouse.

- Naked mole rats live together in large colonies led by a dominant rat 'queen'.

OXYGEN REMINDER

Oxygen makes up around 20% of the air around you. If it fell to 5%, you'd soon faint and your brain would start to die from lack of oxygen (called hypoxia).

Some patients suffer from hypoxia after a stroke or heart attack. Doctors hope to use naked mole rat science to help them.

CLIMBERS AND DIVERS

Too little oxygen in the blood affects mountain climbers at high altitude and can cause breathing failure. Too much oxygen in the blood can cause 'the bends' which affects scuba divers and astronauts if oxygen bubbles build up in their bloodstream. Doctors are studying how these rodents adjust easily to varying oxygen levels, hoping to help climbers and divers. That's big science from a little mole rat!

DID YOU KNOW?

Rodents (from the Latin for 'to gnaw') are mammals with a pair of continuously growing incisors (front teeth). About 40% of mammal species are rodents.

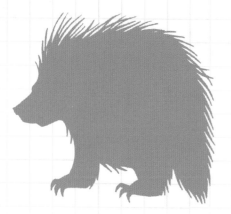

PORCUPINE SCIENCE

Porcupines are the second largest rodent in North America after the beaver. The name means 'quill pig' as porcupines are covered with as many as 30,000 sharp pointed quills. Some quills are almost 30 cm (1 foot) long and usually they lie flat – until a porcupine is scared. Then the quills stand up like a pin cushion! Despite this prickly suit of armour, some animals, like mountain lions and wolves, will risk the porcupine's spikes for a tasty snack.

FACT FILE

- Porcupines have sharp claws for climbing trees.

- They have long, sharp incisors which never stop growing.

- There are more than two dozen species of porcupine worldwide.

- The hair on a porcupine's back, sides and tail is actually soft. However, the sharp quills are mixed in among the hair.

- Porcupines live in deserts, forests and grasslands and eat bark, stems, fruit and leaves.

BRILL QUILL

- Quills have sharp tips and lots of barbs that make them difficult to remove once stuck in a predator. Porcupines grow new quills to replace the ones they lose.

- Each quill has 700 to 800 barbs along its tip.

- Porcupines can easily stab themselves with their own quills. No problem – the quills are tipped with an antibiotic that helps stop infection.

- The porcupine's quills come out of its body quite easily. Predators can end up with a face full of quills. Ouch!

SUPER QUILLS

Porcupine 'quill science' is inspiring developments in surgery. Porcupine quills are super-tough and designed to penetrate skin easily. Scientists are trying to develop less painful hypodermic needles that, like these quills, penetrate skin more easily without bending. They are also looking at ways of using quill design to improve the repair of wounds.

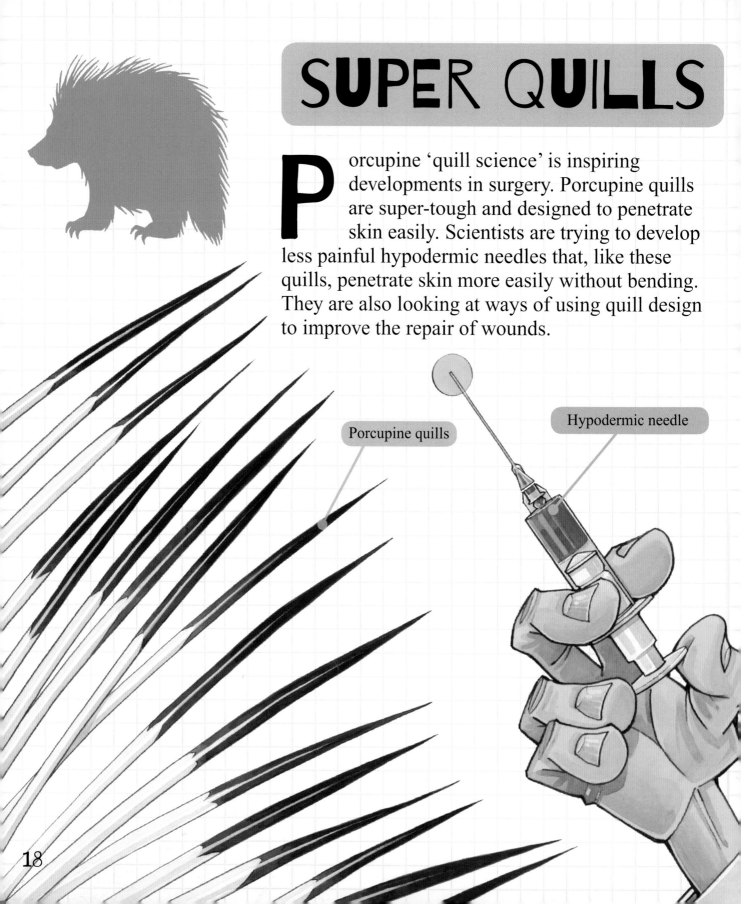

Porcupine quills

Hypodermic needle

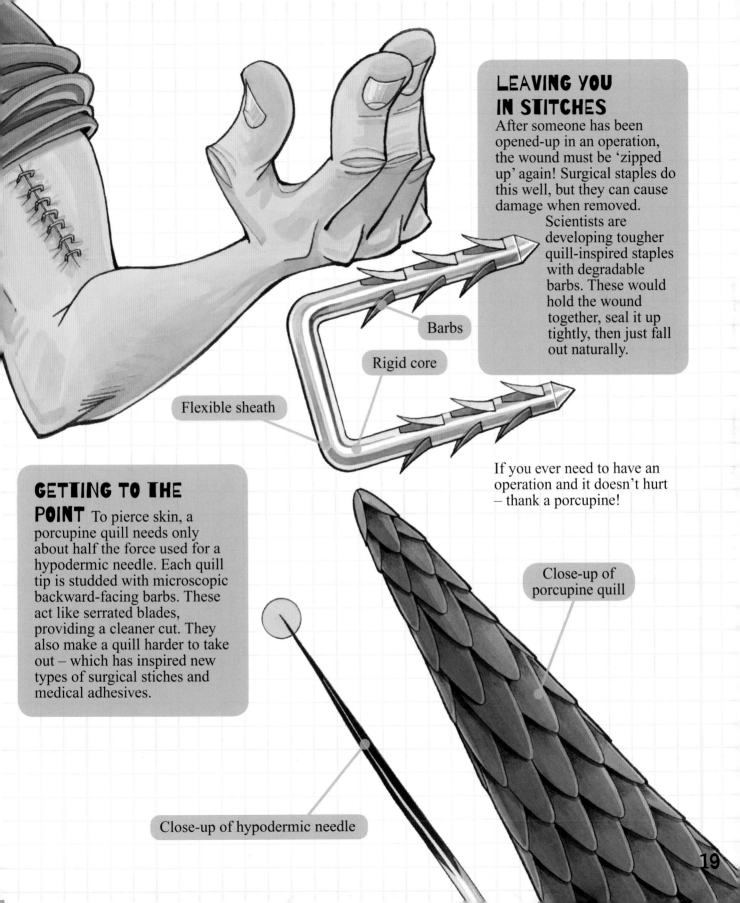

LEAVING YOU IN STITCHES

After someone has been opened-up in an operation, the wound must be 'zipped up' again! Surgical staples do this well, but they can cause damage when removed. Scientists are developing tougher quill-inspired staples with degradable barbs. These would hold the wound together, seal it up tightly, then just fall out naturally.

Barbs

Rigid core

Flexible sheath

If you ever need to have an operation and it doesn't hurt – thank a porcupine!

GETTING TO THE POINT
To pierce skin, a porcupine quill needs only about half the force used for a hypodermic needle. Each quill tip is studded with microscopic backward-facing barbs. These act like serrated blades, providing a cleaner cut. They also make a quill harder to take out – which has inspired new types of surgical stiches and medical adhesives.

Close-up of porcupine quill

Close-up of hypodermic needle

19

SHAPESHIFTING MAMMALS

Armadillos are mammals that are related to sloths and anteaters. They mainly live in South America. They have pointed or shovel-shaped snouts, small eyes and are covered from head to tail in flexible bands of 'armour' made up of overlapping bony shell plates. The three-banded armadillo can roll into a ball to protect itself from danger. Scientists have been exploring useful ways of applying this defensive measure to technology.

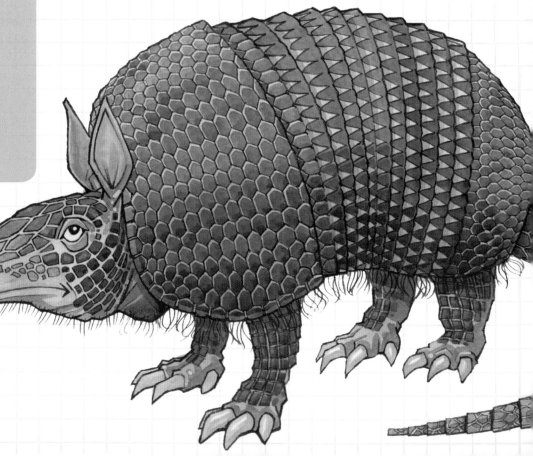

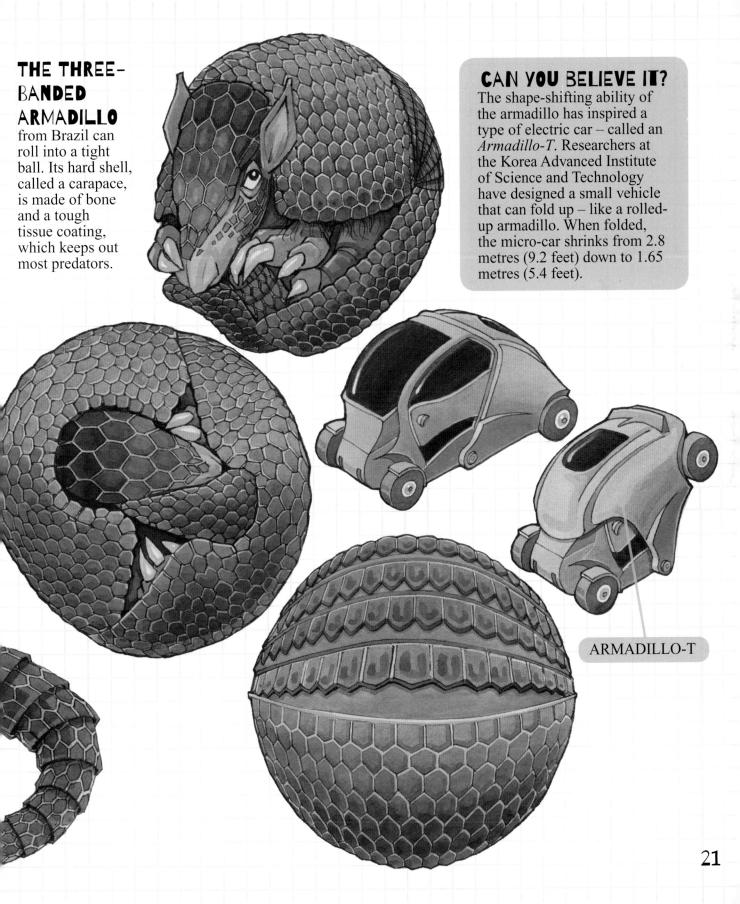

THE THREE-BANDED ARMADILLO

from Brazil can roll into a tight ball. Its hard shell, called a carapace, is made of bone and a tough tissue coating, which keeps out most predators.

CAN YOU BELIEVE IT?

The shape-shifting ability of the armadillo has inspired a type of electric car – called an *Armadillo-T*. Researchers at the Korea Advanced Institute of Science and Technology have designed a small vehicle that can fold up – like a rolled-up armadillo. When folded, the micro-car shrinks from 2.8 metres (9.2 feet) down to 1.65 metres (5.4 feet).

ARMADILLO-T

SUPER DESIGNS

J ust like an armadillo, a pangolin is 'armour-plated' and can roll up to protect itself, but these animals aren't related in any way. The pangolin lives in Africa and Asia and is more like a scaly anteater.

Their tongues are longer than their bodies and ideal for licking up termites. Unable to run fast, and having no teeth, the pangolin relies on its large, overlapping scales for protection.

FACT FILE

- A pangolin's scales are made of keratin (just like our finger nails) and make up about 20% of its body weight.

- The word 'pangolin' comes from the Malay word 'pengguling', which means 'one that rolls up'.

- When threatened, a pangolin can also lash out with its sharp scaly tail and can easily cut a predator's skin. It can also emit a foul smell from its rear end.

- There are eight different pangolin species, ranging from 30cm (1 foot) to 100 cm long (3.28 feet).

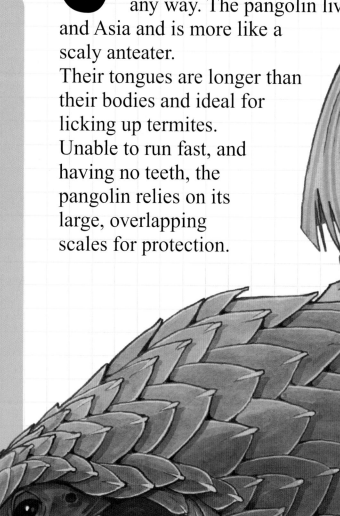

BACKPACK

Like the armadillo, a pangolin's armour is rigid yet flexible, enabling the animal to move freely. New types of sturdy backpack have been inspired by the pangolin's armour.

A GIANT PANGOLIN BUILDING

The pangolin-inspired roof of the Waterloo International Terminal in London has a series of steel arches with over 2,520 overlapping glass panels. These move to allow the surge in air pressure to escape when trains enter the station. This mimics a pangolin's scales which move to let air circulate to regulate its body temperature.

When threatened, the pangolin tucks its head into its stomach and wraps itself into a ball. Nothing can open it.

WHALES AND DOLPHINS

Just like bats, whales and dolphins use sound to find their way around. They make a range of clicks and 'songs' to send sound waves far underwater. These sound waves bounce off any objects or other creatures, giving whales and dolphins detailed information of whatever is around them. The range of their low-frequency sonar is amazing, as they can find tiny objects in total darkness some distance away. They rely on sonar much more than sight to find food, family members or their direction. This echolocation deep underwater is incredible 'sound science'.

FACT FILE

- Dolphins and whales are similar as they are both intelligent marine mammals that use echolocation to communicate and navigate.

- Both whales and dolphins need to breathe fresh air, which they do through blowholes in the top of their heads. Many whales have two blowholes, while dolphins have only one.

- Dolphins are toothed whales and the largest dolphin is the Orca. Often it is mistaken for a whale because Orca are known as killer whales.

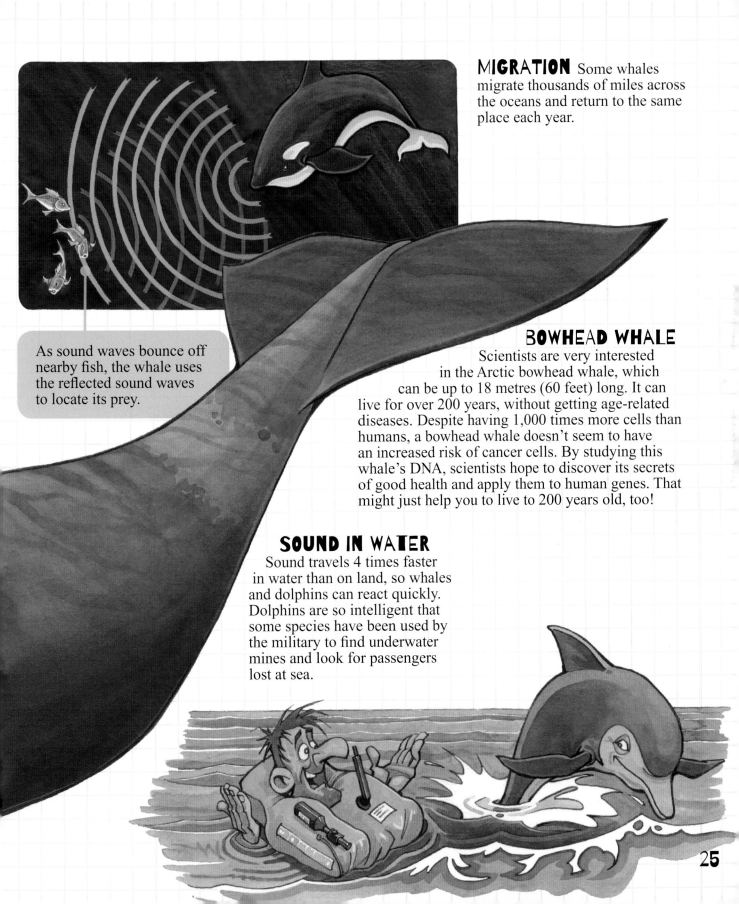

MIGRATION Some whales migrate thousands of miles across the oceans and return to the same place each year.

As sound waves bounce off nearby fish, the whale uses the reflected sound waves to locate its prey.

BOWHEAD WHALE

Scientists are very interested in the Arctic bowhead whale, which can be up to 18 metres (60 feet) long. It can live for over 200 years, without getting age-related diseases. Despite having 1,000 times more cells than humans, a bowhead whale doesn't seem to have an increased risk of cancer cells. By studying this whale's DNA, scientists hope to discover its secrets of good health and apply them to human genes. That might just help you to live to 200 years old, too!

SOUND IN WATER

Sound travels 4 times faster in water than on land, so whales and dolphins can react quickly. Dolphins are so intelligent that some species have been used by the military to find underwater mines and look for passengers lost at sea.

DOLPHIN OCEAN SCIENCE

Dolphin's use of sonar makes them experts at underwater communication. They can recognise specific calls from up to 25 kms (15.5 miles) away – an ability that has inspired technology. A company called EvoLogics has developed a high-performance underwater modem that copies dolphins' unique 'ultrasound'. These modems form the tsunami early warning system across the Indian Ocean, allowing people to be evacuated in advance of the destruction caused by tsunami waves.

DOLPHIN SKIN

Dolphin skin is special. Its smooth elastic structure helps dolphins sense tiny ripples and currents and also keeps parasites off them.

A synthetic coating that mimics dolphins' skin is being used on ships, submarines and boats to reduce drag.

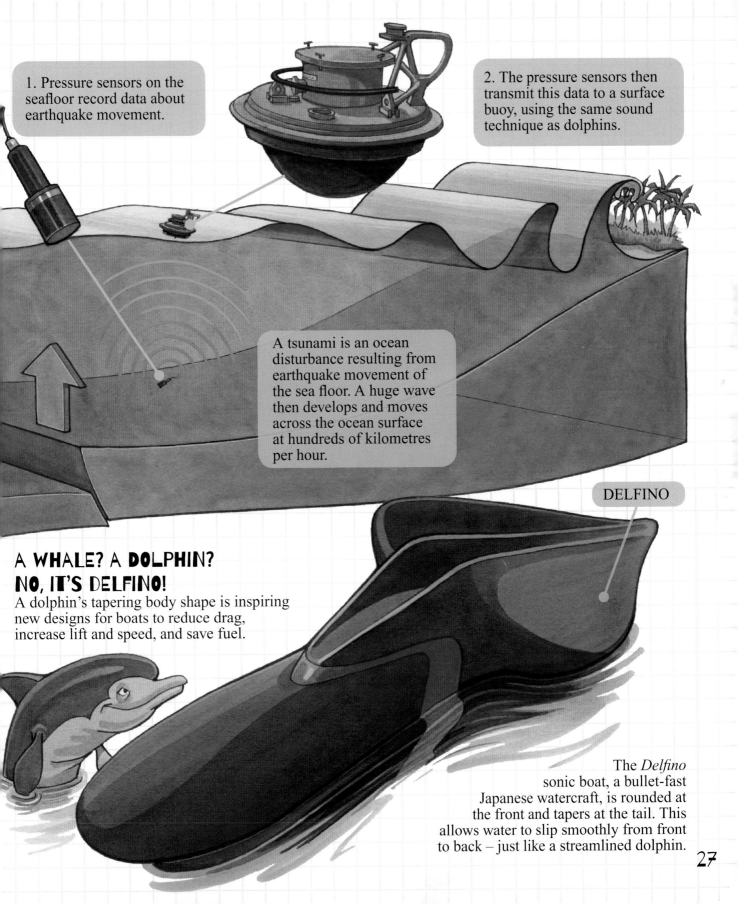

1. Pressure sensors on the seafloor record data about earthquake movement.

2. The pressure sensors then transmit this data to a surface buoy, using the same sound technique as dolphins.

A tsunami is an ocean disturbance resulting from earthquake movement of the sea floor. A huge wave then develops and moves across the ocean surface at hundreds of kilometres per hour.

DELFINO

A WHALE? A DOLPHIN? NO, IT'S DELFINO!

A dolphin's tapering body shape is inspiring new designs for boats to reduce drag, increase lift and speed, and save fuel.

The *Delfino* sonic boat, a bullet-fast Japanese watercraft, is rounded at the front and tapers at the tail. This allows water to slip smoothly from front to back – just like a streamlined dolphin.

27

FLIPPER PHYSICS

Humpback whales are about the size of a school bus and weigh as much as five elephants. It takes ten years for a new-born whale, or 'calf', to grow to its full, adult size. They migrate all over the world with their haunting 'songs'. Their name comes from the large hump that forms as they arch their backs when swimming. They use their flippers and huge tail fin, or fluke, to leap acrobatically from the sea. The hump back's 5-metre-long (16.4 feet) flippers have inspired the world of science and technology.

DID YOU KNOW?

The humpback whale flipper is unique because of the ridges and bumps called 'tubercles' along its edge. Scientists believe they are the key to the whale's effortless movement through water.

You would think all those bumps would cause drag through the water. In fact, in scientific tests, the 'tubercles effect' makes the flippers far more effective than smoother designs.

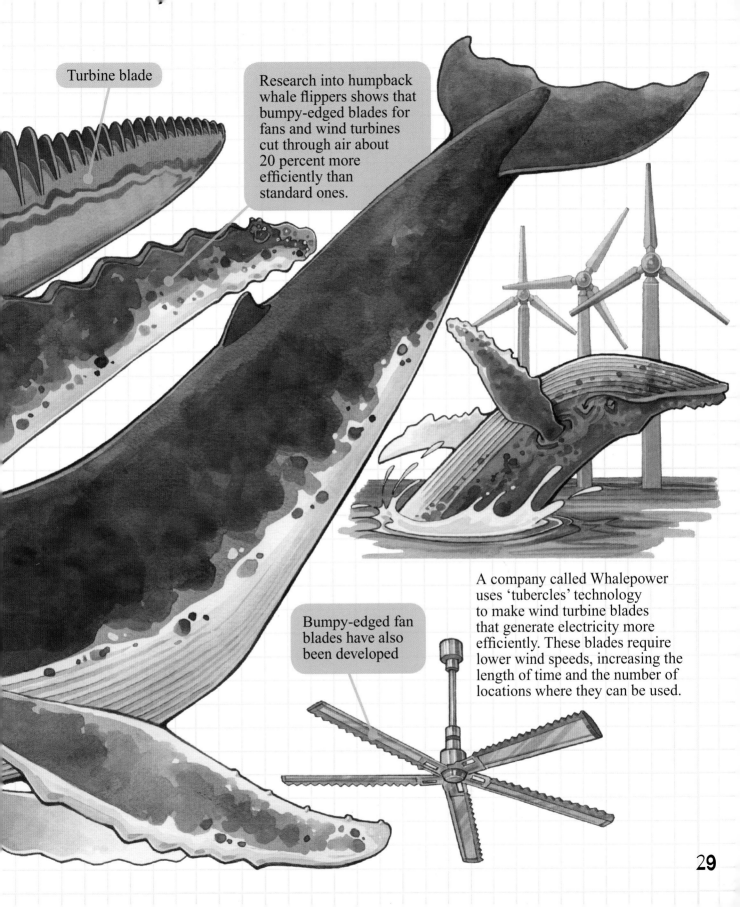

Turbine blade

Research into humpback whale flippers shows that bumpy-edged blades for fans and wind turbines cut through air about 20 percent more efficiently than standard ones.

Bumpy-edged fan blades have also been developed

A company called Whalepower uses 'tubercles' technology to make wind turbine blades that generate electricity more efficiently. These blades require lower wind speeds, increasing the length of time and the number of locations where they can be used.

GLOSSARY

Adhesive a substance for sticking things together, such as glue, cement or paste.

Antibiotic a natural substance or drug that prevents harmful bacteria from causing disease.

Biologist a scientist who studies living organisms and life processes.

Convex curved or rounded like the outside of a circle.

Decibel a unit for measuring the loudness of sounds.

Degradable able to wear away (decompose) naturally.

DNA the special code inside genes that passes on to each generation.

Drone a small aircraft or boat without a pilot and controlled by radio signals.

Echolocation a way of finding an object using sound waves that reflect off it back to the sender.

Genes sets of instructions in all our body cells that make us who we are.

Hypodermic being able to inject beneath the skin.

Incisor a front tooth for cutting (between the side canine teeth in a mammal).

Keratin a type of protein that makes up hair and hard tissue such as fingernails.

Manoeuvrability being able to move about easily and skilfully.

Membrane a thin layer of a plant or animal part.

Nocturnal active at night.

Omnivore an animal or a person that eats both plants and meat.

Parasite a living thing which lives in or on another living thing.

Physics the science of matter and energy and the relationships between them.

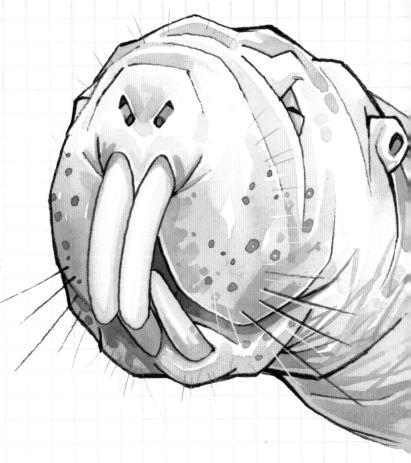

Predator an animal that lives by killing and eating other animals.

Prey an animal hunted or killed by another animal for food.

Saliva liquid produced in the mouth that helps the swallowing of food.

Serrated a jagged edge, like on a toothed blade.

Sonar emitting sound pulses and gaining information when they are reflected.

Surveillance investigating by watching details very closely.

Tubercle a knobby lump or outgrowth on a plant or animal.

Ultrasound high frequency sound (over 20,000 Hz), the upper limit of human hearing.

INDEX